#2 in the Molly Learns Series

Molly Learns 10 Facts About Theodore Roosevelt

By
Marla Harms Judge
and Molly the History Dog

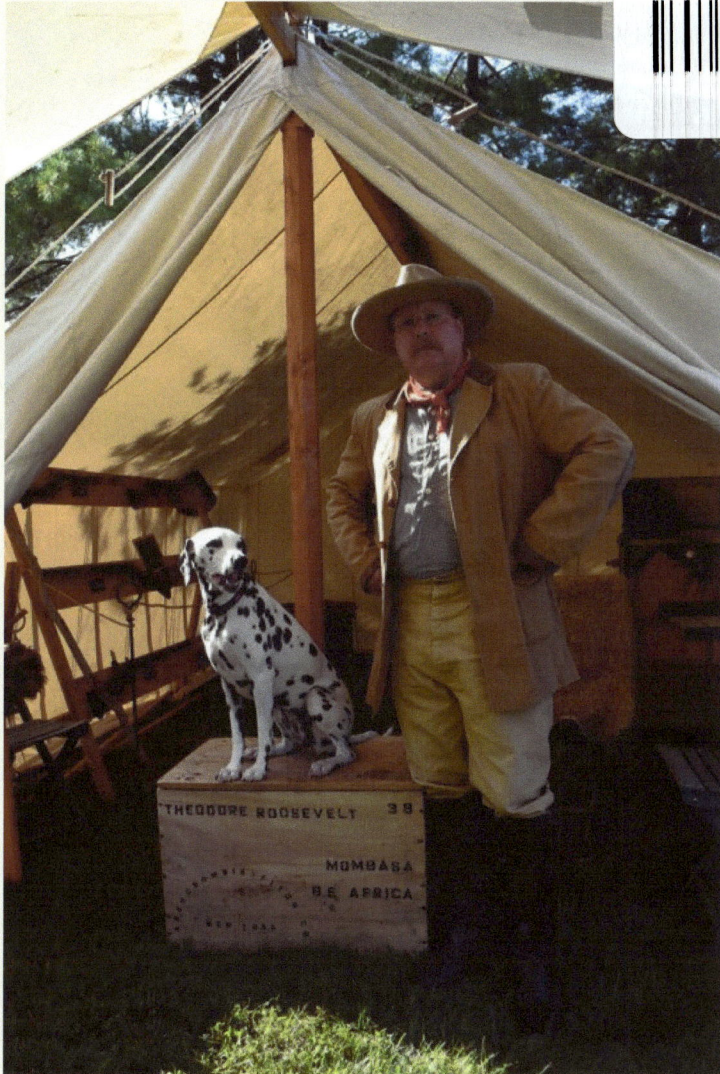

I visit with a historical reenactor
portraying Theodore Roosevelt.

Book design by Madeline Littleton

ISBN Paperback 978-1958533208
ISBN Hardcover 978-1958533116
Library of Congress Control Number: 2022920662

Please write to us at: Mollythehistorydog@gmail.com
Visit: mollythehistorydog.com

Crippled Beagle Publishing, Knoxville, TN, USA
crippledbeaglepublishing.com

"Believe you can
and you're
halfway there!"
Theodore Roosevelt

Hi! My name is Molly.
I am a dalmatian dog.
I am white with black spots.
Did you know that some
dalmatians have brown spots?

Have you ever seen a dalmatian?
When dalmatian puppies are born,
we are pure white. We don't get our
spots until we are about 10 days old.

I pose with my favorite teddy bear!

5

Theodore Roosevelt

My human family and I like to travel and learn about famous people and places.
I have lots of fun!

Today I want to tell you 10 facts I learned about a famous American.
He was a cowboy and a soldier before he became the 26th President of the United States of America.
Can you guess who he was?

Did you guess Theodore Roosevelt?
If you did, you guessed right!

The 26th President of the United States of America was Theodore Roosevelt!

OCTOBER 1858

Sunday	Monday	Tuesday	Wednesday	Thursday	Friday	Saturday
					1	2
3	4	5	6	7	8	9
10	11	12	13	14	15	16
17	18	19	20	21	22	23
24	25	26	27	28	29	30
31						

8

One of the first facts I learned is that
Theodore was born October 27, 1858.
He was born in New York City.
Have you ever been to New York?
I have not. New York is a long way
from where I live.

This photo shows the house where Theodore was born.

New York is a big, busy city. When Theodore was born, there were no cars for people to drive. They walked or rode in carriages pulled by horses. Would you like to ride in a horse-drawn carriage?

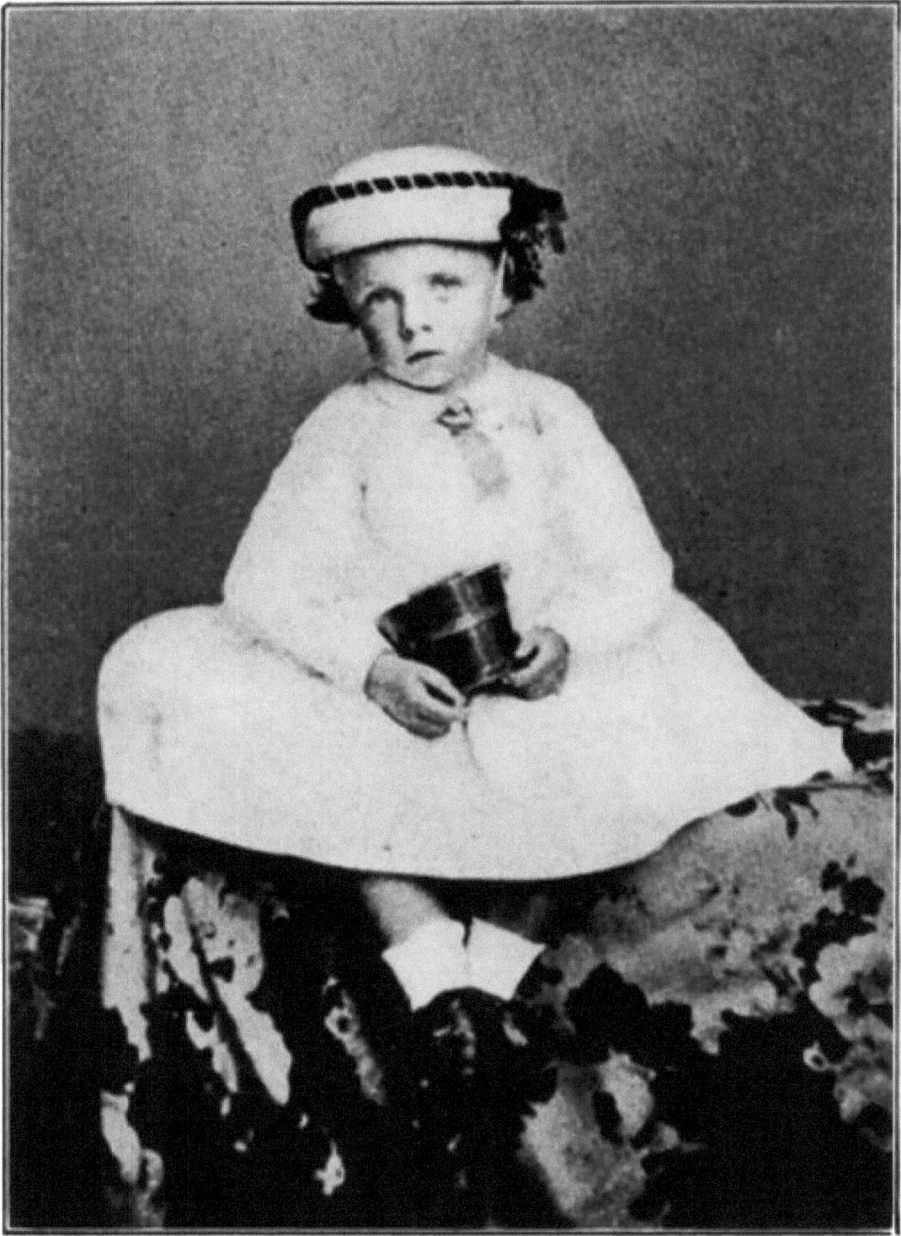

Theodore looks unhappy to pose for this picture.

Theodore had several nicknames as he grew up.
When he was little, his family
called him "Teedie." As he got older, he became
"Teddy." As an adult, he liked to be
called "T.R.," "Colonel," or "Mr. President."

"I was a sickly, delicate boy, suffered much from asthma, and frequently had to be taken away on trips to find a place where I could breathe. One of my memories is of my father walking up and down the room with me in his arms at night when I was a very small person."
T. Roosevelt

When Teddy was a little boy, he was sick a lot.
He had an illness called asthma.
Do you know anyone who has asthma?

Theodore as a little boy.

I learned that when you have asthma it is
sometimes hard for you to breath. I think that
would be scary! Teddy's father would take him
for carriage rides when he had an asthma
attack to try to find better air for him to
breath. They did not have medicine for him to
take like they do today!

No matter where Theodore was, he always found time to read!

"I am part of everything I read."
T. Roosevelt

I was sad to learn that when Teddy was not feeling well, he would spend many long days in bed. To pass the time he would read. Teddy loved to read. He read many, many books. He learned about people, geography, culture, history, and more.

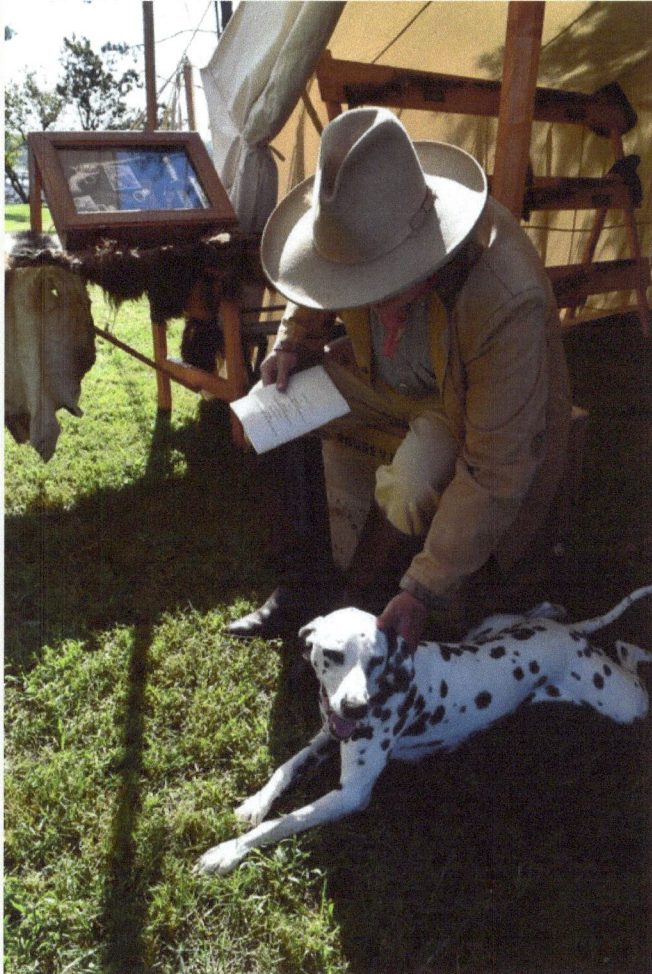

I had a lot of fun with Adam, who portrays Theodore. Here he is reading me a story.

When he got older, Teddy would read a book every morning before breakfast. At night before bed, he would read two or three more! Do you have a favorite story to read? I like stories about DOGS.

Historical reenactors portray Mr. & Mrs. Roosevelt

"I am pretty happy, for I have come to the
conclusion that I have got mighty
nice children, all of them!"
T. Roosevelt

Theodore with his family.

Theodore was married and had six children. That is a big family! How many people are in your family? His children were Alice, Theodore Jr., Kermit, Ethel, Archibald, and Quentin.

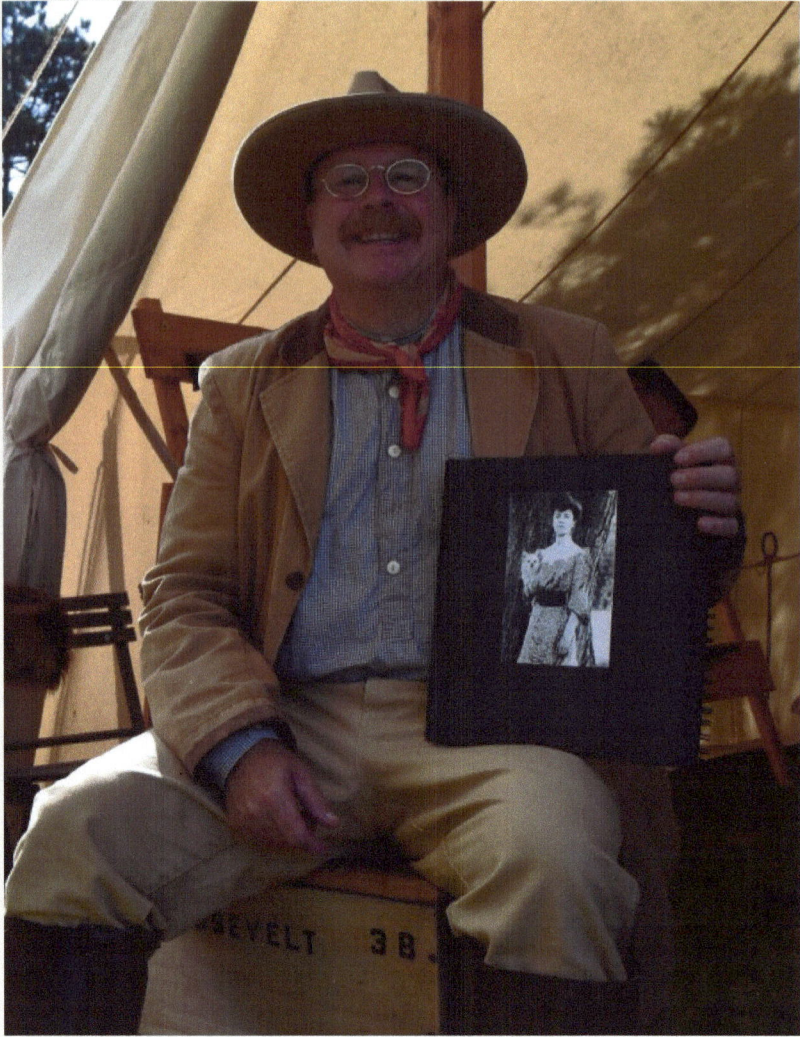

I heard many stories about the mischief the Roosevelt children got into!

All of the children were mischievous, but Alice in particular liked to misbehave. When Theodore was the president, someone told him he should have better control of Alice. He said, "I can be President of the United States, or I can control Alice. I cannot possibly do both!"

Did you know that many presidents have had unusual pets when they have lived in the White House? The White House has been home to donkeys, a bobcat, tiger kittens, a racoon, and an alligator!

One fact I was very happy to learn was that the Roosevelt family liked animals! When they lived in the White House, they had a miniature zoo. Their pets included a small bear, dogs, rabbits, owls, guinea pigs, chickens, and snakes!

Roosevelt's one-legged chicken!

A garter snake like the Roosevelts' Emily Spinach.

They even had a one-legged chicken! Alice liked to walk around with her snake, Emily Spinach, in her pocket or on her arm. Many people do not like snakes and tried to stay away from Emily Spinach. Do you like snakes? I don't think I like them very much.

I do have a favorite story about President Roosevelt's children when they lived in the White House. Remember, they could be very mischievous. One day Archie Roosevelt was in bed with the measles. His brother Quinten decided that a visit from his pony would help Archie feel better

The mischievous children make a picture with several pets.

Archie rides Algonquin on the White House lawn.

Quinten put the pony Algonquin on the
elevator and took him up to Archie's room!
President Roosevelt got a call about a pony
in the White House. He thought it was
hilarious.

The Roosevelt family lived on the
third floor of the White House.
To get the pony up to the bedroom
Quinten had to convince the animal to
get on the elevator.
The White House staff was not
happy to see a pony prancing through
the beautiful building.

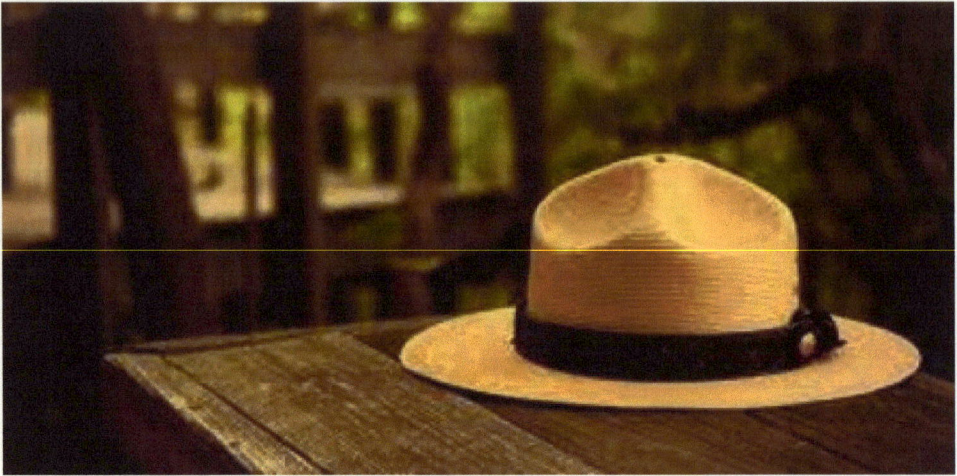

Park Rangers work hard to preserve our country's history and beautiful lands. The iconic "flat hat" is part of their uniform.

The National Park Service has 423 sites it cares for. They help to preserve nature and our country's history!

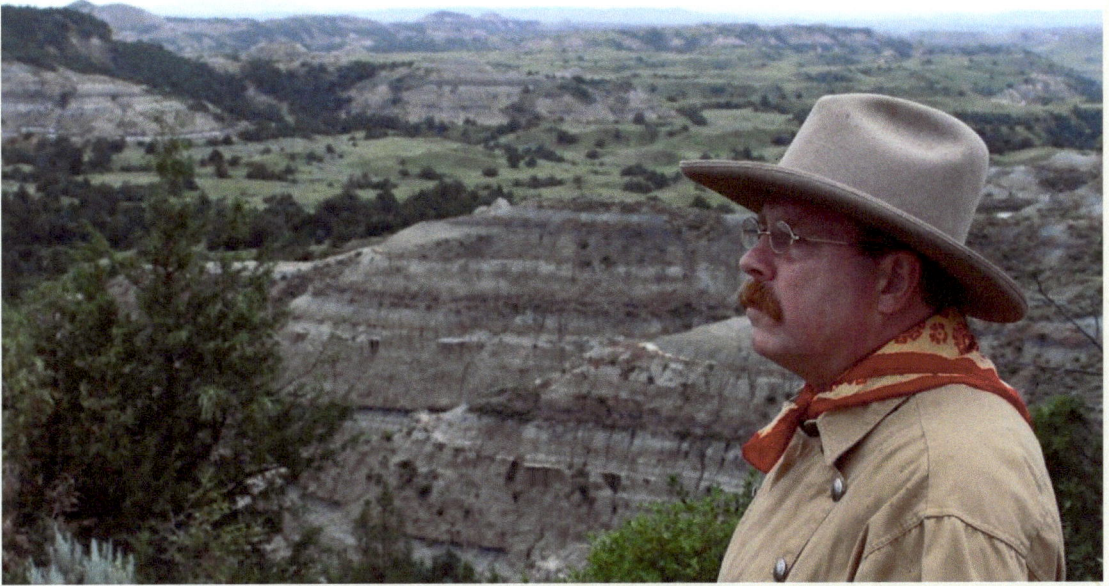

A historical reenactor visits one of our beautiful national parks.

Have you ever visited one of our national parks?

They are spectacular! President Theodore Roosevelt helped make sure that land was protected and the parks were created.

Roosevelt visits a national park.

Theodore visits one of the national parks he helped form.

One of his favorite parks to visit was Yellowstone National Park. He helped form the National Park Service so that the unique beauty and history of our country would be saved for all of us.

I love to travel and see new places. Where would you like to visit on vacation?

Have you heard the story of how the teddy bear got its name? One time, when Theodore and friends were hunting, they saw a bear tied to a tree. Theodore refused to hurt it, so the other people with him began calling the bear a "Teddy Bear." Soon, stuffed bears everywhere were called teddy bears!

This is a modern teddy bear. It is my favorite toy to snuggle with!

A historical reenactor tells the story about the teddy bear.

Do you have a teddy bear? I like to snuggle with mine.
(Sometimes I chew on him, but he does not mind.)
How cool is it that teddy bears are named
for one of our presidents?

Before Theodore was the president, he was a
soldier. He led a group of soldiers call the Rough
Riders. I don't think I would want to be a soldier,
but I am glad so many men and women go and
fight for our country.

Colonel Roosevelt, proud to serve our country.

The Rough Riders were a group of
volunteer soldiers who went to
Cuba to fight for the United States during
the Spanish/American War.
Theodore became their Colonel.
After the war, he still liked to be
called Colonel.

Colonel Roosevelt stands at the Rough Rider's camp.

Do you know anyone who is a soldier, marine, sailor, or airman? They are incredibly brave. Colonel Roosevelt was proud of the time he volunteered to serve in the army.

T.R. enjoys working as a cowboy on his ranch.

Theodore was also a cowboy before he became president. He traveled out to what is now North Dakota. He bought a ranch and raised cattle. One time he tracked down cattle rustlers who stole some of his cows.

Have you ever visited a farm or a ranch? I like to see all the animals. I think I would like to be a cow dog. Would you want to be a cowboy or a cowgirl?

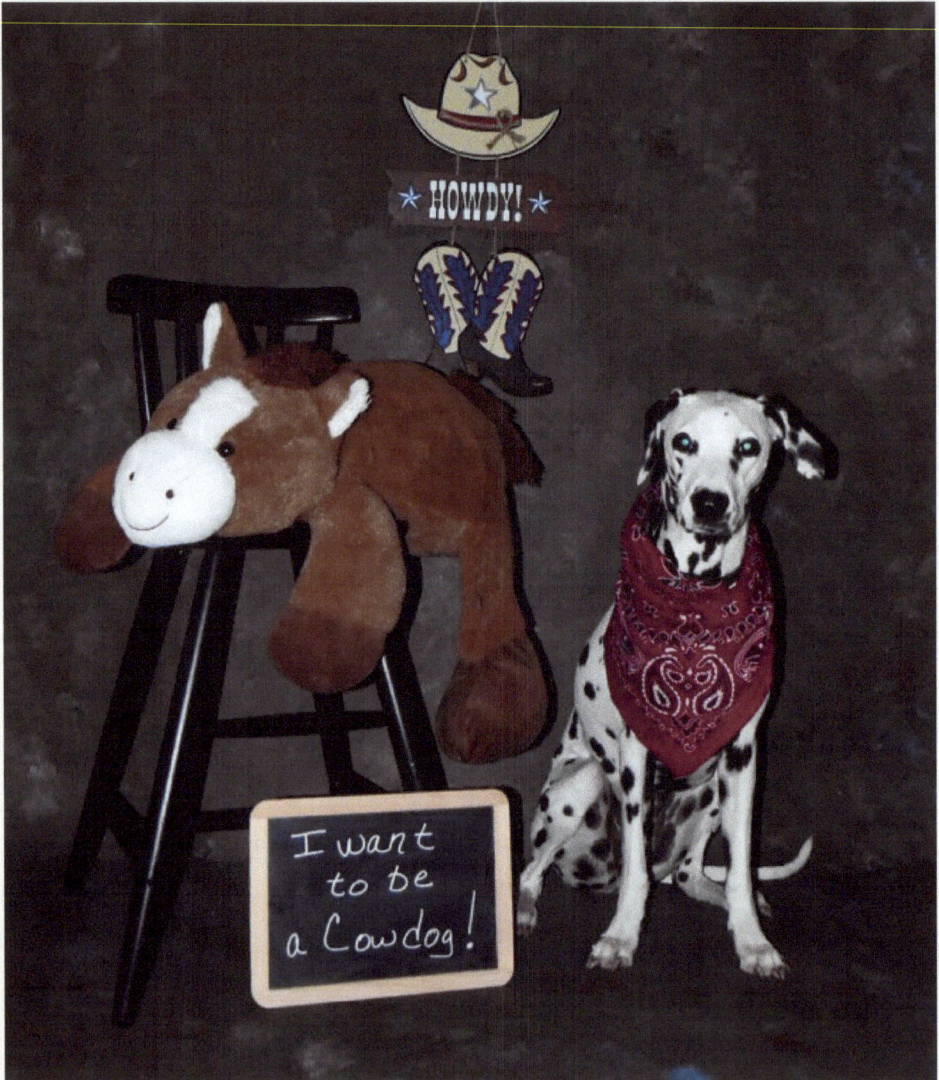

I am ready to be a cow dog.

Theodore was an adventurous man.
He traveled to many places around the world.
Some of his adventures lead him to
do amazing things.

Are you brave? Would you want to ride
in an airplane made like the one
President Roosevelt rode in?
Would you go underwater in a submarine?
I am not sure I would.

While Theodore was president, he did many things no other president had ever done before. I think he was brave to be the first president to take a ride in an airplane. That airplane looks rather frightening!

President Roosevelt's first plane ride.

Theodore Roosevelt rode in this submarine named USS Plunger.

He was also the first president to ride in a submarine! President Roosevelt liked to try new experiences. He was adventurous.
He would be an interesting person to know.

Did you count as you read my book? Did you learn 10 facts about Theodore Roosevelt? These are the facts we talked about:

1. When and where Theodore Roosevelt was born.

2. Theodore had asthma.

3. Theodore loved to read.

4. The Roosevelt family was large.

5. The family had many pets.

6. Algonquin the pony visited inside the White House.

7. Theodore helped form our National Parks.

8. The Teddy Bear was named for Teddy Roosevelt.

9. Theodore was a Rough Rider and a cowboy.

10. President Roosevelt had many presidential firsts.

Which story was your favorite? Did you learn anything new about Theodore Roosevelt that you didn't know before? I hope so!

Love,
Molly

About the authors!

Molly is a wonderful dalmatian dog. She lives with her family in a big old house with a big yard to run and play in.

Marla Harms Judge lives with her husband Robert and Molly. Marla and Robert have three children, five grandchildren, and one great grandson. Marla has worked as a school librarian, a park ranger, and a living history interpreter. She loves reading and history.

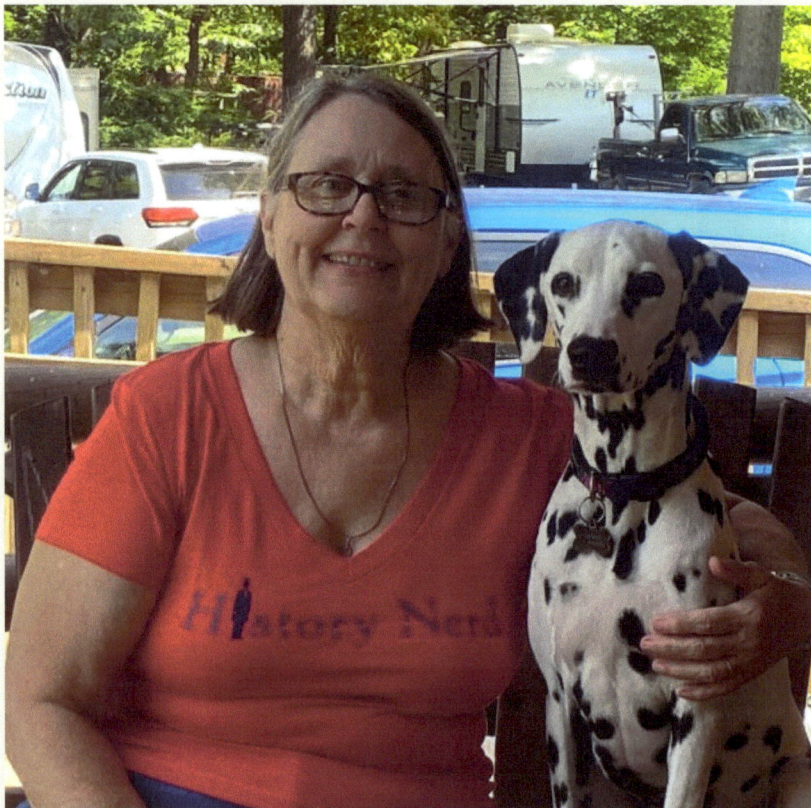

Molly and Marla want to say thank you to Robert for all of his love and support!

Other books by Marla Harms Judge

Mrs. Lincoln's Birthday Surprise

Will and Tad Lincoln try to find the perfect
birthday gift for their Ma.
Maybe a frog?
Mr. Lincoln saves the day and helps the boys.

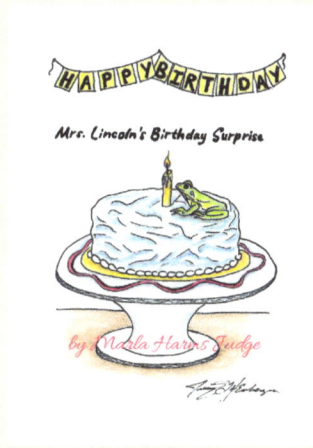

Molly Learns 10 Facts About Abraham Lincoln
#1 in the Molly Learns Series

Visit us at www.mollythehistorydog.com.

<u>**Historical Reenactors:**</u>
Adam Lindquist (www.teddyrooseveltlive.com)
Margaret Lindquist

<u>**Places to visit to learn about President Theodore Roosevelt:**</u>

Sagamore Hill National Historic Site
20 Sagamore Hill Rd, Oyster Bay, New York 11771

Theodore Roosevelt National Park
Box 7
Medora, North Dakota 58645

Theodore Roosevelt Birthplace National Historic Site
E 20th St., New York, New York 10003

In the future:
Theodore Roosevelt Presidential Library
Medora, North Dakota
Opening in 2025

Photo Credits

Cover – Taken in Springfield, Illinois

Pg 1 – Marla Judge

Pg 5 – Marla Judge

Pg 6 – Library of Congress (LOC)

Pg 10 – LOC

Pg 11 – www.Gutenberg.org

Pg 13 – LOC

Pg 14 - LOC

Pg 15 – Marla Judge

Pg 16 – Adam Lindquist

Pg 17 – LOC

Pg 18 – Marla Judge

Pg 20 – LOC/Public Domain

Pg 21 - LOC

Pg 22 – LOC

Pg 24 – National Park Service

Pg 25 – Adam Lindquist

Pg 26 – LOC

Pg 27 – LOC

Pg 28 – Marla Judge

Pg 29 – Adam Lindquist

Pg 31 – LOC

Pg 32 – LOC

Pg 33 – LOC

Pg 34 – Marla Judge

Pg 36 – LOC

Pg 37 – LOC

Pg 40 – Marla Judge

Pg 44 – Marla Judge

Color this happy picture of a little girl and her Teddy bear.

www.ingramcontent.com/pod-product-compliance
Lightning Source LLC
Chambersburg PA
CBHW042056040426
42447CB00003B/241